KNOWING DIABETES

Dr. A.K. Sethi
(M.B.B.S., F.C.C.P.)

V&S PUBLISHERS

Published by:

V&S PUBLISHERS

F-2/16, Ansari Road, Daryaganj, New Delhi-110002
☎ 011-23240026, 011-23240027 • *Fax* 011-23240028
Email info@vspublishers.com • *Website* www.vspublishers.com

Regional Office Hyderabad
5-1-707/1, Brij Bhawan (Beside Central Bank of India Lane)
Bank Street, Koti, Hyderabad - 500 095
☎ 040-24737290
E-mail vspublishershyd@gmail.com

Branch Office Mumbai
Jaywant Industrial Estate, 2nd Floor–222, Tardeo Road
Opposite Sobo Central Mall, Mumbai – 400 034
☎ 022-23510736
E-mail: vspublishersmum@gmail.com

Follow us on: 🇹 f in

All books available at **www.vspublishers.com**

Printed at : Repro Knowledgecast Limited, Thane

Preface

D iabetes is a dreaded disease which is known to mankind from time immemorial. In India there are about 35 million people who are suffering from diabetes. This accounts for about 25% of total diabetic patients in the world. Majority (90%) of these individuals suffer from type 2 diabetes which is usually detected accidently or in advanced stage. The World Health Organisation (WHO) has estimated that by the year 2025, the population of diabetic people in the world would reach 300 millions (presently 150 millions) and in India 57 millions. WHO has declared India as the Diabetes capital of the world.

Majority of Indian individuals suffer from the misconception that diabetes is due to excess intake of "Sweet Items" and will be "Cured" if they stop their intake. Moreover, diabetes is a disease which can be controlled but rarely cured by modern medicines. This book tells the readers the complications diabetes creates in the body.

In order to provide all this information for a layman, I have ventured to write this book and hope the readers will find it very useful and enjoyable to read.

Contents

1. What is Diabetes?

D iabetes or Diabetes Mellitus is a disease in which the patient passes increased quantity of urine. Diabetes is derived from two Greek Words "dia" which means "through" and "betes" which means, "to pass". "Mellitus" is another Greek word, which means "sweet". In this disease the patient passes large quantities of urine containing a sweet substance, namely glucose. It is either due to lack of production of a hormone called insulin in the pancreas or due to the inefficient action of insulin.

Structure and Function of Pancreas

Pancreas is an important structure found in the abdomen, which plays a major role in the causation of Diabetes Mellitus. Pancreas is a soft, flat gland, which is 15-20 cm long, 3-5 cm broad, 2-4 cm thick and 80-90 gm in weight. It is situated in the posterior part of abdominal cavity just behind the stomach. Pancreas consists of three parts—the head, the body and the tail.

The head is enclosed in a C-shaped concave structure, the duodenum that lies between the lower end of stomach and the upper end of small intestine. The tail ends in a firm

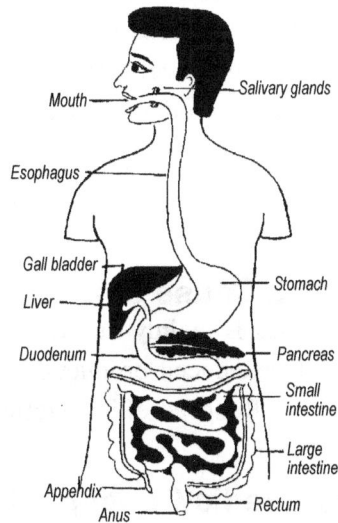

Fig. 1.1:
Pancreas & surrounding organs

7

organ, the spleen that is located in the left upper portion of abdominal cavity. The portion between the head and the tail is the body.

Functionally the pancreas consists of two parts:

The Digestive Part
About 99% of the pancreas consists of the digestive part. It comprises a large number of cells which produce the digestive enzymes which are important for the digestion of proteins, carbohydrates and fats in the food we eat.

The Hormonal Part
About 1-2% of the weight of the pancreas constitutes the hormonal part. A hormone is a chemical substance which is produced by an organ or a gland and sent to another part of the body through the blood where it increases the functional activity of that part. The hormonal part of the pancreas consists of large clusters of cells called the islets of Langerhans, named after the discoverer Paul Langerhan who discovered them in 1869. There are about two million islets in the pancreas. The islets consist of 4 types of cells:

A or alpha cells produce the hormone glucagon.

B or beta cells produce the hormone insulin.

D or delta cells produce the hormone somatostatin.

F cells produce pancreatic polypeptide.

Insulin is the most important hormone whose deficiency is responsible for producing the disease Diabetes Mellitus.

Basic Cause of Diabetes
Diabetes is mainly due to two causes:
1. Reduced production of Insulin.
2. Reduced efficacy/effectiveness of Insulin.

Ayurvedic Concept of Diabetes
In order to understand the Ayurvedic concept of Diabetes we must first understand the 3 bodily elements, which are responsible for sustaining the living body in their normal state.

These 3 elements are:

1. "Dosha"
2. "Dhatu"
3. "Mala"

Any imbalance in the 3 elements produces disease or ill health.

"Doshas" govern the physical and chemical functions of the body.

They are of 3 types:

1. "Vata"
2. "Pitta"
3. "Kapha"

1. "Vata" is responsible for active movements of different organs and parts of our body.

There are 5 types of Vata:

- **Prana** refers to functions of the brain and nervous system i.e. sensations of smell, taste, touch, hearing and vision, movements of upper and lower limbs, rectum and sex organs and breath.

- **Udana** refers to movements of the chest, diaphragm and voice box. It controls movements of breathing out, sneezing and speech.

- **Samana** refers to movements of the intestine along with digestion and absorption of food substances.

- **Apana** refers to the movements of the bladder, rectum, uterus and is important for passing urine, stools, menstrual fluids, semen and foetus (delivery).

- **Vyana** is concerned with movements of all kinds of both voluntary and involuntary muscles. It is responsible for movements of the heart e.g. blood vessels, lymph (special white fluid present in different parts of the body) glands and glands which produce hormones.

The diseases caused by the disorder of Vata are as follows:

- Asthma
- Epilepsy (fits) and other mental disorders
- Urticaria (a skin disease)
- Viral fever (due to temperature changes)
- Anaemia (lack of iron in blood)
- Obesity (Increased weight gain)
- Diabetes
- Diarrhoea or constipation
- Reduced functions of thyroid and adrenal glands

2. "Pitta" is responsible for the chemical reactions that take place in our body. It is of 5 types:

- **Pachaka** is due to digestive enzymes and other chemicals in the body, which control the digestion and absorption of food substances.

- **Ranjaka** is responsible for haemoglobin (the iron-containing pigment in blood) production.

- **Alochaka** is responsible for the biochemical activity of the eye, which is responsible for perception of vision.

- **Sadaka** is responsible for normal functions of the mind.

- **Brajaka** is responsible for removing waste products in the form of sweat and enhancing the natural glow of the skin.

The diseases caused by disorders of Pitta are as follows:

- Toxic fevers
- Hyperacidity (Gastritis)
- Vomiting
- Diarrhoea
- Jaundice
- Anaemia (due to destruction of bood cells)
- Bronchitis

- Skin diseases associated with pus formation
- All infections due to toxins, bacteria, viruses etc.

3. Kapha refers to promotion of growth brought about by secretions of different types of the body and organs. It is of 5 types:

- **Kledaka** refers to secretions of the mouth, stomach and intestines, which dissolve the food and destroy bacteria.

- **Avalambika** refers to secretions of the respiratory tract from the nose to the lungs and facilitates passing of air and flushes out foreign substances.

- **Bodhaka** is the watery secretion of the glands around the taste buds of the tongue which help in perceiving the taste.

- **Tarpaka** refers to the cerebrospinal fluid which is a secretion surrounding the brain and spinal cord. It provides nutrition to the brain and protects it from toxic substances.

- **Shleshaka** is the fluid lying in the bones and joint spaces called as synovial fluid producing movements of bones and joints with ease. The watery fluid surrounding and protecting the heart, and lungs are also referred to as Shleshaka Kapha.

The diseases caused by disorders of Kapha are as follows:

- Common cold.
- Infection of the lungs and other parts of respiratory system.
- Diarrhea due to infection.
- Jaundice.
- Eczema, pimples and other skin infections.
- Arthritis (painful joints).
- Rheumatic heart disease.
- Swelling and infection of the kidneys (glomerulonephritis).
- Peritonitis (swelling of abdominal cavity).
- Encephalitis, meningitis and other infections of the brain.
- Benign tumours of different parts of body.

Dhatu is a substance which is responsible for formation of basic structure of body. There are 7 types of dhatus i.e. lymph, blood, muscle tissue, fat tissue, bone-marrow, sperm or ovum.

Malas are waste products of various dhatus produced during the course of metabolic changes in the body. Examples of malas are sweat, urine, stool, gases, bile, ear-wax, nasal discharge, mucous secretions etc.

Thus disease is the imbalance of doshas, dhatus and malas.

Diabetes is one Type of disorder of the urinary tract in which patients pass excessive and turbid urine (PRAMEHAS).

There are 20 Types of Pramehas which are classified according to the doshas into 3 major types:

Vataja Pramehas—which are 4 in number.

Pittaja Pramehas—which are of 6 types.

Kaphaja Pramehas—which are of 10 types.

Diabetes (Madhumeha) is a type of Vataja Prameha.

■ ■ ■

2. Types of Diabetes

Diabetes Mellitus is divided into different types, depending on the cause of disease and the situation in which it develops. Each type is distinctly different from the other by virtue of the cause of the disease, its presentation, complications, diagnosis and treatment. The different types of Diabetes Mellitus are discussed below.

Insulin Dependent Diabetes or Type 1 Diabetes

This type of diabetes is commonly known to occur during early childhood and adolescence. This is sometimes also known as Juvenile Diabetes due to this reason. It can also occur in middle aged and older individuals. In this disease, the pancreas produces very little or no insulin due to which the patient has to depend on artificial source of insulin. It develops suddenly and progresses rapidly. By the time it is diagnosed the patient may have developed many complications in the body. It is not commonly present in other family members. The individuals who develop this disease are usually not obese and have a normal dietary pattern and an active lifestyle. These individuals respond only to insulin injections and if not treated properly they develop complications and outcome may sometimes be fatal. The disease is more common in Europe and America. It affects 1 in 500 children and 1 in 200 adolescents.

Non-Insulin Dependent Diabetes or Type 2 Diabetes

This type of diabetes is seen in middle-aged adults and older individuals. This disease is more common than Type 1. It develops slowly and gradually and may not be noticed for years together. It is commonly detected when a person goes for a medical check-up before joining employment or before an operation. Such individuals are obese/overweight, voracious eaters and have a sedentary life-style. Often such people have other family members especially parents, grand parents, uncles, aunts or siblings with the same disease. The disease is not as serious as Type-1, with fewer complications developing and patients respond to oral medicines, diet restriction and exercise. The major differences between the two Types of diabetes are outlined below:

Differences Between Type 1 and 2 Diabetes

	Feature	Type 1 Diabetes	Type 2 Diabetes
1.	Age group	Commonly occurs during childhood and adolescence	Occurs in middle-aged and older individuals.
2.	How detected	Commonly detected only when complications have developed	Detected during official medical check up or before an operation
3.	Progress of disease	Develops suddenly and rapidly	Develops gradually and progresses slowly.
4.	How common	Less Common	More Common
5.	Body-weight	Usually normal	Increased
6.	Eating habits	Not contributory	Voracious eaters
7.	Lifestyle	Active or sedentary	Sedentary
8.	Family history	Family members not affected	Family members normally affected
9.	Treatment	Insulin injections are necessary	Normally controlled with oral medicine
10.	Complications	Develops early	Develops late

Diabetes due to Diseases of the Pancreas

Since the main cause of diabetes is the production of insulin in the pancreas, any disease affecting it will indirectly give rise to diabetes. The common disease/disorders of the pancreas are as follows:

a) Any infection of the pancreas

b) Tumour related to the pancreas

c) Any obstruction between pancreas and other organs due to stone, toxic chemicals etc.

d) Removal of pancreas by operation.

Such individuals may develop the disease at any age irrespective of their body weight, eating habits, life style and family history. They commonly require insulin injections for treatment while some may respond to oral medicines.

Diabetes due to Malnutrition

In developing countries like India many individuals in the adolescence and adulthood develop diabetes due to severe malnutrition. These people are commonly deprived of food in early life especially protein-rich food. Due to this they are undernourished and very lean and have very little production of insulin hormone.

Due to lack of food the insulin which is produced is also insensitive since it has no proper foodstuff to act on. Thus these individuals slowly devlop diabetes. They normally respond only to artificial sources of Insulin.

Diabetes due to Other Hormones

Some individuals develop diabetes due to excessive production of certain hormones which interfere with the normal action of insulin e.g. growth hormone, thyroid hormones, glucagon (from pancreas). Due to their interference, insulin fails to carry out its normal activities on the foodstuffs and patients develop high levels of blood sugar and hence diabetes. The features of such patients are variable and also their treatment.

Diabetes due to Medicines and Toxic Chemicals

Certain medicines and toxic food substances and rodenticides are capable of destroying the pancreatic cells, which produce insulin. This gives rise to diabetes.

Diabetes due to Liver Diseases

Certain infections, obstruction and other metabolic disorders related to liver also give rise to diabetes.

Diabetes in Pregnancy

Some pregnant women have been observed to develop diabetes during their pregnancy.

The different types of diabetes according to Ayurvedic system of medicine are given below:

Types of Diabetes According to Ayurveda

Diabetes is classified in two ways:

- Based on the Type of doshas. (Ref. Chapter 1)
- Based on inheritance. (heredity)

Based on Type of Doshas	Based on Inheritance
1. Vataja Type	1. Inherited
2. Kaphaja Type	2. Non-Inherited
3. Pittaja Type	a) Due to over-weight
	b) Due to under-weight

The Ayurvedic concept of diabetes is based on the imbalance of the 3 doshas, namely vata, pitta and kapha. When the vata dosha is predominant the type is called vataja and similarly pittaja and kaphaja types. Based on the inheritance theory the disease could be an inherited type in which there is diabetes in one of the blood-relatives, irrespective of the weight of the individual. In the non-inherited type we have 2 sub types: one which is seen in overweight individuals who are voracious eaters and have a sedentary lifestyle and the other subtype where the person is under-weight and malnourished due to lack of proper intake of food or chronic diseases like tuberculosis.

■■■

3. What Causes Diabetes?

Diabetes is a disease, which is due to multiple factors related to the individual and the environment and involves many systems of the body. Hence it is a multi-factorial and multi-system disease.

The various factors which contribute to the development of this disease are as follows:

Age

Although diabetes may occur at any age irrespective of the type, the majority of cases are seen in middle-aged and older individuals. Insulin Dependent (Type 1) and malnutrition-related diabetes occur in younger age group. In the latter group, the complications are more common, treatment difficult and outcome is sometimes fatal. Some researchers have also declared aging, as an important factor for diabetes and senile changes in the pancreas could also be contributory.

Sex

This disease is equally distributed in both sexes though in some countries, the male diabetics are more while in others, the females are more. The disparity could be due to lack of notification of this disease in hospitals since private practitioners treat many patients.

Diet and Nutrition

In obese individuals, Type 2 Diabetes was common due to resistance of body to normal insulin due to excess fat cells. People with malnutrition commonly have very little amount of insulin in the body and hence suffer from Type 1 or Insulin Dependent Diabetes Mellitus. Of late, research has shown that Diabetes may occur irrespective of nutritional status. Some studies have shown that children who are given cow's milk early in infancy may develop type 1 Diabetes. This is due to presence of "Bovine Serum Albumin"—a substance which may damage the insulin producing cells in the pancreas. Excessive carbohydrates, especially refined sugars may indirectly lead to type 2 Diabetes by giving rise to obesity.

Lifestyle

Lifestyle of individuals can prove to be a risk factor for development of diabetes in two ways:

Sedentary Lifestyle

People who have minimum physical activity or a sedentary life style are very much susceptible to develop Non-insulin Dependent Diabetes. The lack of exercise alters the action of insulin and its receptors.

Urbanized Lifestyle

Statistical evaluation of prevalence of diabetes in developed vs. developing countries and rural vs. urban population has shown interesting findings. People migrating from developing to developed or rural to urban areas show increase in the prevalent rate of diabetes.

Thus urbanized or westernized lifestyle promotes development of diabetes.

Infections

Infections both due to bacteria and viruses can precipitate diabetes in susceptible individuals. Infection of the pancreas can produce a series of events resulting in destruction of beta cells of pancreas, which produce insulin.

Medicines and Toxic Substances

Certain medicines e.g. steroid hormones and substances which increase the excretion of urine (diuretics) have been known to produce diabetes. Studies in animals using toxic substances e.g. Alloxan, Streptozotocin, Rat Poison (Valcor) have produced diabetes. Certain food substances e.g. Cassava and certain beans when taken in large amounts are capable of producing toxic effects on insulin producing cells due to high content of cyanide in them.

Alcohol when taken in large quantities over a prolonged period can prove to be toxic to the liver and pancreas and can promote obesity.

Stress Factors

Stress of any kind can precipitate diabetes in susceptible individuals. Stress may be in the form of surgery, infections, injury, pregnancy or mental tension due to different reasons.

Inheritance

The importance of inheritance in diabetes is seen in the following ways:

- Diabetes especially Type 1 is more commonly seen in the parents and blood relatives of diabetics than in general population.
- Certain markers - Human Leukocyte Antigen (HLA) when present in individuals signal the presence of diabetes especially Type 1.
- Many individuals with Diabetes especially Type 2 have other associated problems like obesity, hypertension and high blood levels of fat.
- Certain individuals have a defective mechanism by which the beta cells get destroyed by some self-destructive process.

Causes of Diabetes According to Ayurveda

According to the Doshas

Any imbalance in the amount of doshas in the body gives rise to diabetes. If the vata dosha is increased and the others are decreased, the type of diabetes is known as Vataja madhumeha.

Similarly in cases of increase in Pitta and Kapha doshas, the types are respectively Pittaja and Kaphaja.

Dietary Factors

Ayurveda has always implicated the cause of a particular disease due to ingestion of particular food substance. In the case of diabetes too, ayurvedacharyas have implicated increased intake of high carbohydrate and fat diet as the cause of diabetes.

People who have an increased intake of food substances like milk and its products, honey, sugar, wheat, rice, bajra, grains, meat, fish, eggs, ghee, oils, tea, coffee, aerated drinks and ice-cream are prone to develop diabetes.

Lifestyle

Sedentary lifestyle: People who are affluent doing more of mental work than physical e.g. politicians, shopkeepers, executives, zamindars, teachers, doctors and lawyers are very prone to develop diabetes. In contrast labourers, farmers, policemen, soldiers etc. carrying out more of physical activity are less prone to develop this disease.

Urbanized/westernized lifestyle: Due to the rapid urbanization and western influences, many people are ambitious, carrying on with irregular and high-caloric food and poor bowel and bladder movements and spending a luxurious life.

These people are highly prone to develop diabetes.

Lack of Exercise

Excess intake of carbohydrates and fat along with lack of exercise and laziness gives rise to increased body weight, which predisposes diabetes.

Nutritional Status

Malnutrition as well as obesity are risk factors for diabetes.

Psychological Factors

Mental stress, anxiety, depression and other psychological illnesses can also precipitate diabetes.

Heredity

Diabetes may be inherited from parents, grandparents and blood relatives.

Other Factors

Increased sexual activity, chronic diseases like tuberculosis (TB), piles, venereal diseases etc also give rise to diabetes.

■■■

4. Signs and Symptoms of Diabetes

The features (signs and symptoms) of diabetes are variable and depend on the following factors:

- Type of diabetes
- Stage of diabetes
- How it presents itself-abruptly or gradually
- Age of the patient
- Presence or absence of complications of the disease

Patients with uncomplicated diabetes may present to the doctor with one or more of the following complaints/symptoms:

- Passage of large volumes of urine, which is dilute and pale in colour.

- Passage of urine at night even in the absence of high fluid intake.

- Urine may contain "sugar" (glucose) which is not normally present in other individuals.

- Abnormally intense thirst, which leads to drinking of large quantities of water and fluids, irrespective of weather conditions.

- Sudden development of a voracious appetite.

- Complain of getting tired easily and a sensation of "weakness".

- In spite of increased appetite, loss of weight instead of weight gain.
- White marks on the clothes which are not easily washed off.
- Itching and redness around the genitals.
- Diminished vision with frequent changes of spectacles due to short sight.
- Slow healing of wounds as compared to normal people.
- Tingling (Pins and needles sensation) and numbness (diminished sensation) in hands and feet.
- Pain in the lower limbs especially the calf muscles which is not relieved by routine painkillers.
- Repeated infections of the skin, respiratory tract or urinary tract.
- Impotence.

■ ■ ■

5. Complications of Diabetes

Understanding the features of diabetes is incomplete without knowing the complications caused by the disease, how they present themselves and their treatment. Knowing the complications is important because Type 1 Diabetes always heralds its arrival along with complications. Type 2 Diabetes also gives rise to complications in the long run.

When a person is declared to have diabetes by his doctor the person receives a setback. He may think "why me of all the people? Many people enter into a depressive state with sadness and disturbance of sleep, appetite and concentration. Thus diabetes is a dreaded disease, a phobia and a curse for many.

Why Diabetes is Considered a Dreaded Disease

- It has very few premonitory symptoms before it is detected.
- It can only be controlled, never cured by modern medicines.
- If untreated or otherwise, it can lead to many complications.
- A diabetic feels socially insecure due to his dietary restrictions, regular meals and medications.
- A diabetic is not able to carry out stressful activities as compared to a non-diabetic.

The complications involve many systems and organs and occur due to various reasons. Their presentation varies according to the type of disease, the stage when detected, the organ involved and the extent of control of the blood sugar.

When do Complications of Diabetes Occur?

- When the person is suffering especially from Type 1 Diabetes.
- When treatment is not begun.
- When dosage of medicines/injections is less or more than required
- When treatment is not taken regularly.
- When patient is not responding to treatement.
- When regular blood sugar or other screening tests are not done.
- When the disease is present for a long period especially Type 1.

The complications which are commonly associated with diabetes are as follows:

Hypoglycemia or low blood sugar, ketoacidosis, heart disease, kidney disorders, eye complications, nerve complications, infections, gangrene of foot, and digestive system disorder.

Hypoglycemia or Low Blood Sugar

Hypoglycemia refers to the fall in blood sugar to the level of **50-60 mg/100ml or less**. It may be mild and self-limiting in patients of Type 2 Diabetes who are on oral medications. In contrast it can present as a serious emergency in Type 1 Diabetes patients who are on insulin injections.

The causes of low blood sugar in diabetic patients are summarized below:

- Due to a high dose of insulin injection or tablets.
- Due to error in calculating the dose.
- Starting with a higher dose in the early part of disease.

- Due to improvement in diabetes control.

- Due to reduced requirements after a stress is over or after an infection or delivery.

- When food is not taken immediately after injections or omitted completely.

- After severe exercise.

- In the presence of gastric, liver or kidney disease.

- If certain painkillers are taken along with oral medicines (tablets).

- In infants of diabetic mothers.

Features of Low-Blood Sugar

Features of low-blood sugar vary from patient to patient, with the adult experiencing symptoms earlier than children. The various features of the low-blood sugar are as follows:– increased appetite, vomiting sensation, sweating, feeling of weakness, tingling and numbness of lips and fingers, trembling, pounding heart, headache, blurring of vision or double vision, increased yawning, twitching of muscles, irritability or sadness or confusion or aggressive behaviour, and if not controlled or very severe, drowsiness, fits or loss of consciousness.

Diagnosis

- The diagnosis of this complication can be done by simple blood sugar estimation. It will reveal blood sugar level below 50mg/100ml. If some treatment is given bef ore the blood sample is taken, the blood sugar level will be normal.

- The features of the disease and their disappearance immediately after treatment also clinch the diagnosis.

- Urine never contains sugar during this complication.

Treatment

Once hypoglycemia is suspected, the patient has to be given some carbohydrate containing food immediately and repeated once the blood sugar level report is available. Any of these substance may be given—a cube of sugar, 10-20 gm of glucose powder - Glucon-C, Glucon-D, Dextrose, Electral etc., fruit, bread, biscuit or Glucose in the liquid form may be given through the blood (by intravenous drip) depending on the seriousness of the situation.

- For complicated cases with fits, coma, abnormal behaviour, hospitalization is essential.

Prevention

- Patients and their relatives or guardians should learn to identify the warning symptoms of low blood sugar and act accordingly.
- They should report to their consulting doctors about these episodes and seek advice regarding change in dose or timing of medicines.

Patients should take their insulin injections or oral tablets just a few minutes before or during a meal.

If the meal is skipped or delayed for a long time low blood sugar will definitely occur.

- Oral medicines should never be taken along with alcoholic drink.
- If a strenuous exercise is done, it should be followed by some extra carbohydrate food item.
- All diabetic patients must carry an Identity card prepared by the Diabetes Association of India. It should contain name, address telephone number, doctor's name and address. The following appeal is normally written in the card:

"I am a diabetic patient.

If I am drowsy or behaving abnormally please give me sugar or sweet drink.

If I am unconscious please take me to a hospital or a doctor."

Along with this appeal the medicines and their doses are also given in the card.

The identity card saves the person's life in a case of emergency. Moreover many patients who develop low blood sugar and as a consequence exhibit abnormal behaviour, have been arrested on charges of being drunk and disorderly. Prolonged state of low blood sugar can permanently damage the brain.

Ketoacidosis

In uncontrolled diabetes due to deficiency of insulin, there is increased breakdown of fats leading to formation of ketone bodies in large quantities in blood and urine. Their elevated levels also lead to increased acidity of blood and tissues. Hence the term ketoacidosis.

Before the discovery of insulin, more than 50% of diabetic patients used to die due to ketoacidosis. Now less than 20% of diabetics in India die from Diabetic Ketoacidosis. The commonest cause of death is the ignorance on the part of patients and sometimes even the doctors to appreciate the danger signals of this complications arising out of uncontrolled disease.

Ketoacidosis is slightly more common in younger individuals especially of the fair sex and also those who are thin. It is also less common in India, Africa, Japan and West Indies probably due to low fat and high carbohydrate diets consumed in these countries.

The causes or provoking factors, which lead to this complication, are given below:

The patient omits or reduces the dose of insulin due to:

- Ignorance of its consequences.
- Non-availability of doctor for injecting the dose.
- Religious fasting or otherwise.
- Non-availability of food.
- Due to infections of the throat, lungs, skin, urinary system etc.
- Vomiting or diarrhoea due to dietary or other factors.
- Ineffective or inadequate dose of insulin injection.

28

- In newly diagnosed Type 1 diabetes patients as the first symptom.
- In stressful situations like pregnancy, injury, during an operation etc.

Features of the Disease

These are very few warning signals of this condition in the early phase of disease. Mostly the disease develops gradually except in the case of children. The common features of ketoacidosis are as follows: Intense thirst, passing increased volume of urine, vomiting, headache, loss of appetite, restlessness, weakness, pain in abdomen (cramps), constipation, drowsiness, and in late stage deep and rapid breathing, acidotic breath (odour of over ripe fruit), cool clammy skin, dry tongue, rapid and feeble pulse and ultimately coma.

Diagnosis

Besides the above features, a few laboratory test will confirm the diagnosis. The tests are as follows:

- Blood sugar levels are very high ranging upto 800mg/100ml or more.
- Urine contains sugar and ketone bodies.
- Blood is acidotic with low values of bicarbonate.

Treatment

The patient has to be urgently treated in the hospital. He may require the following:

- Insulin injections.
- Water and electrolytes replacement through venous blood (drip) to compensate water loss and acidity.
- Antibiotic injections to control infection.

Prevention

- Regular and timely intake of medicines and insulin.
- In case of stressful conditions and infections, dosage to be increased after consulting the doctor.

- If any unusual symptoms develop.
- Immediately inform the doctor.
- Take bed rest.
- Take plenty of fluids to prevent loss or deficiency of water and salts.
- If diagnosis is confirmed, patient has to be immediately rushed to hospital. If patient is already in coma, delay in treatment will make recovery very difficult.

Differences in coma due to low blood sugar and ketoacidosis is given in the table below:

Differences Between Coma due to Low Blood Sugar and Ketoacidosis

	Coma with low blood sugar	Coma with ketoacidosis
1.	Develops all of a sudden.	Develops after ill health for several days.
2.	Due to excessive dose of insulin injection.	Due to no insulin or less dose.
3.	Lack of food or missing meals.	Too much food intake.
4.	Increased appetite.	Decreased appetite.
5.	Abnormal behaviour.	Absent.
6.	Tingling and numbness of lips and fingers.	Absent.
7.	Heart beat normal.	Heart beat increased.
8.	Increased thirst and urination absent.	Present
9.	No acidotic or fruity odour of breath.	Present
10.	Breathing normal.	Increased breathing.
11.	Pulse is strong.	Pulse is weak.
12.	Abdominal pain and constipation absent.	Present.
13.	Urine does not contain glucose on ketone.	Urine contains glucose and ketone.
14.	Blood sugar levels low.	Blood sugar levels increased.
15.	Treatment by giving food	Treatment by insulin injections.

Diabetes and Heart Disease

Diabetic individuals are more prone to develop heart disease as compared to non-diabetic individuals.

The danger signals of heart disease in diabetics are easy fatigability (person gets tired easily), increased breathlessness on minimal exertion or even rest., chest pain in the centre or towards left side of chest, sudden uncontrolled blood sugar, and increase in the blood pressure.

Treatment of heart disease is always done in the hospital with regular monitoring of various body and laboratory parameters.

Prevention of Heart Disease in Diabetics

- Regular check-up of blood sugar and proper control with medicines.
- Monthly monitoring of blood pressure.
- Quarterly or half-yearly tests of heart function-ECG, blood tests.
- Prevent weight gain by promoting salt restricted, fat-free diet and regular exercise.
- A special test of fat content "Lipid Profile" if available may be done. It indicates the magnitude of risk of individual developing heart disease.
- Smoking and drinking of alcohol to be stopped.
- Oral pills in diabetic women to be used with caution.

Diabetes and Kidney Disorders

As in the case of heart, long-standing diabetes can also lead to complications in the kidneys. Patients with Type 1 Diabetes have 30-40% chance of developing kidney disorders after 20 years while it is 15-20% in Type 2, but since Diabetes Type 2 is more prevalent, kidney disease is more prevalent in Type 2 than Type 1.

In India 11% of deaths in diabetics are due to kidney disorders.

The mechanism of development of these disorders is same as that of the heart. There is deposition of fat on the walls of small and large blood vessels (arteries) of the kidney leading to narrowing of blood vessels and blood flow obstruction. Due to this defect, the blood pressure increases and waste products of the blood accumulate.

The danger signals of kidney disorders in diabetes are increased lassitude, breathlessness on exertion, increased urination at night, swelling of the ankle, unstable control of blood sugar (reduced insulin requirements), and increased blood pressure.

Diagnosis

- When kidneys are functionally normal, the urine contains no protein, while in diseased kidneys, urine contains protein which may rise upto 5gm in 24 hours or even more.

- When disease is advanced in stage, blood levels of urea and creatinine are very high.

- Due to diseased kidneys, urinary infection may develop as evidenced by pus cells and bacteria in urine.

Treatment

- Proper control of sugar by regular blood sugar monitoring and medicines.

- Treatment of high blood pressure if present.

- Treatment of urinary infection if present.

- In advanced disease of kidney, dialysis (removal of waste products from blood and re-circulation of purified blood) or kidney transplant may be required.

Prevention

Following measures in diabetics can prevent this disease:

- Regular monitoring of blood pressure and control whenever necessary.

- Regular monitoring of blood sugar and controlling it.

- Avoid medicines (e.g. painkillers, dyes for x-rays) which affect kidney function.

- Regular 24 hours urinary protein levels and blood tests for kidney function (blood urea and creatinine).

Complications of the Eye in Diabetes

When diabetes is present for a long time, the following complications of the eyes are likely to develop:

- Blindness due to damage to blood vessels of innermost part of eye-the retina.
- Cataract (Motia-Bind) or opacity of the lens of the eye.
- Myopia or short-sight where the person cannot see distant obejcts.
- Glaucoma (Kala-Motia) or increased pressure in the eye producing blurring of vision and sometimes blindness.

Blindness due to Retinal Damage

Diabetics have 25 times more risk of developing blindness than non-diabetics. After 10 years of diabetes 50% of patients develop blindness due to retinal damage which increases to 80% after 15 years.

About 10% of blind population in U.K. and U.S.A is diabetic.

Salient features of this disease are as follows: Patients with Type 1 and Type 2 diabetes are equally prone to develop this complication. The blindness is present in different age group and sexes. It may occur in one eye or both. Cause of blindness is reduced blood circulation in blood vessels of eyes due to increased fat deposition with resulting leakage of blood from friable (weak) vessels into the eye producing swelling and later blindness. In early part of the disease there is no symptom. In late disease patient complains of blurring of vision. The disease can only be diagnosed by examining the retina using an ophthalmoscope.

Treatment

- In early part of disease no treatment is required. By controlling blood sugar, blood pressure and reducing fat levels in blood, the disease can be totally controlled.
- In late part of disease treatment is by Laser Photocoagulation or by operation of the retina.

Prevention of Blindness in Diabetics

The blindness in diabetics can be prevented by the following measures:

- Eye examination every 6 months or 1 year after diabetes is diagnosed.
- Avoiding smoking or using tobacco in any form.
- Correction of high blood pressure by medicines and salt-restricted diet.
- Control of blood sugar by regular medicines and blood tests.
- Control of fat levels in blood by regular blood tests and fat-free diet.

Complications of the Nerves in Diabetes

Majority of patients with diabetes develop complications of the nerves. About 60% patients with about 25 years duration of diabetes are found to develop these complications though the number may increase upto 90% in many cases. These complications are detected in both Type 1 and Type 2 Diabetes and mainly in middle-aged or elderly individuals. Invariably they are seen in uncontrolled mild diabetes of long duration.

The nerves involved may be nerves of the hands and feet or those of the brain and spinal cord.

Causes of Damage to the Nerves

- Direct damage due to lack of carbohydrate metabolism.
- Due to reduced blood supply to the nerves.
- Due to deposition of fat in large and small arteries supplying the nerves of hands and feet or brain:

Symptoms of Nerve Damage in Diabetics

The spectrum of symptoms reported by patients with nerves complication are given below:

- Burning, cramp-like, piercing or dull aching pain in the feet and legs rarely in hand especially at night.

- Tingling, numbness or coolness in feet and legs followed by pain in muscles and insensitivity to hot, cold and pain sensations.
- Inability to maintain balance of body and strength and direction of movements of hands and feet.
- Deformities of toes and nails, thickened skin and ulcers on sole (due to insensitivity of feet to repeated injuries).
- Pain, weakness and thinning of muscles of thigh.
- Inability to control passing of urine.
- Repeated diarrhea or constipation.
- Abdominal cramps.
- Inability to sweat.
- Intolerance to extreme temperatures.
- Impotence.
- Fall in blood pressure on suddenly standing up from lying down position.
- Sudden attack of weakness or paralysis usually on one side of body (Stroke).
- Infections of the brain.

Diagnosis is made by nerves conduction studies (velocities) of affected nerves and Electromyography.

Treatment varies according to the presenting feature. Vitamins have no role in treatment.

Prevention

Proper evaluation of symptoms given above. Tests of nerve and muscles function as given above.

Infections

It is universally known that diabetes are very prone to develop infections of different types. About 8.5% of diabetic patients are known to die due to infections inspite of availability of various antibiotics.

The 3 major causes of infections are poor control of diabetes, reduced immunity or resistance to fight diseases, and defects in the blood vessels and nerves.

Types of Infections

- Urinary infections are commonest and increase during pregnancy.
- Chest infections like tuberculosis and pneumonia.
- Skin infection—Boils, carbuncles, fungal infections especially in the genital area in females.
- Rarely infections of bones and gall bladder.

Treatment involves control of blood sugar levels and proper antibiotics.

Gangrene of Foot

Gangrene refers to death or decay of a part of body.

Gangrene of the foot is very common in diabetes and has necessitated amputation (removal) of toes or even the whole foot in many cases.

Causes of gangrene destruction of nerves of the foot or lower limb are reduction in blood supply to the foot and skin infection of the foot or sole.

Symptoms of gangrene are initially pain in the foot affected, later loss of sensations in the foot, changes in the colour and texture, initially red then pale and finally black, coldness in the ankle and foot and skin infection of foot.

Treatment

- Controlling blood sugar is of utmost importance.
- Soft pad on the sole.
- Rest to the legs or complete bed rest.

- Treatment of infection with antibiotics.
- Treatment of pain with pain-killers.
- Amputation (removal) of affected toes or whole foot when disease is spreading or pain not controlled.

Prevention

- Regular monitoring of blood sugar.
- Examination of the feet yearly or twice a year.
- Washing feet daily and using lubricating creams, oils.
- Not to walk barefoot.
- Avoid extremes of temperature.
- Wear appropriately fitting shoes.
- Cut toe nails regularly.
- Never to cut corn or calluses.
- Treatment for skin diseases.

Digestive System Disorders

Some patients with diabetes may present with symptoms of digestive system due to nerve disturbances, which reduce movements of stomach and intestines or reduction in the blood supply or as a part of keto-acidosis.

Symptoms commonly reported are pain in the abdomen, vomiting, diarrhoea or constipation, loss of appetite, passage of smelling, fatty, sticky, stools and fullness of stomach after meals.

Treatment depends on the symptoms.

■■■

6. Diagnosis of Diabetes

he diagnosis of diabetes may appear to be simple and involve just demonstration of increased sugar levels in blood and sometimes in urine, but many facts and fallacies have to be understood.

Diabetes should be suspected in the following individuals:

Criteria for Suspicion of Diabetes

- In persons aged 40 years and above.
- With a history of diabetes in a blood relative.
- Excessively overweight.
- Persons with symptoms like increased thirst, appetite and loss of weight, inspite of good food intake, frequent infections, unexplained weakness.
- Persons with heart disease, high blood pressure or vague pains in the body.
- Women who have put on excessive weight during pregnancy.
- Women who have delivered a baby weighing more than 3.5kg.
- Multiple deaths of babies before or after birth.

The following tests are done to diagnose diabetes and to monitor progress of the disease with medicines.

Urine Examination

- Urine is examined for detection of glucose (sugar) and ketones.
- There are many tests, which are used for this purpose.

Benedicts' Test

This is the oldest test used to detect diabetes. It has of late become obsolete and is used only in remote primary health centres, where facilities for other tests are not available.

In a test-tube 8 drops of urine are mixed with 5ml (one teaspoonful) of Benedict's Qualitative Solution and boiled and colour noted. The results are interpreted as given below:

Results of Benedict's Test

Blue	Nil
Clear green	0.1%
Turbid green	0.3%
Green and yellow precipitate	0.5 to 1%
Yellow	1%
Orange	2%
Brick red	More than 2%

Fallacies of this Test

- It only gives a crude idea of diabetes, because it reveals presence of sugar only when blood sugar increases more than 180mg% i.e. in cases of severe diabetes.

- Even if other sugars i.e. fructose, galactose, maltose and lactose are found in urine, the test gives positive results.

- Certain medicines like aspirin, penicillin and other antibiotics and Vitamin C can also give positive results.

- In children collecting urine sample is difficult.

Dip-stick Methods

There are certain paper or plastic strips coated with chemicals that change colours according to sugar and ketone concentration. For example, one type of strip ranges from yellow through green to dark blue and another from blue through green to brown. The dip-stick is dipped in fresh urine or directly through the urine stream and within 30 seconds the reagent (chemical) side of paper is compared with corresponding colour chart given on the container. Various such dip-sticks are available in the market namely Diastix, Ketodiastix, Gluketur, Uristix etc.

Disadvantages

- It is costly, though cutting the strip longitudinally can reduce cost.

- Patients with colour blindness may misinterpret the results.

- Vitamin C and other medicines may interfere with the results.

The strips have a limited shelf life, especially after the container is opened.

Advantages

- It is a very simple procedure.

- Even the patient at home can do it.

- Result is instantaneous.

- It is useful for monitoring diabetes control at home. Patients with Type 1 Diabetes should check their urine samples 3 to 4 times a day and Type 2 once preferably 2 hours after a meal.

Tests for Ketones in Urine

Ketones in urine can be detected by following tests:

- Dip-stick Method—explained above

- Rothera's Test

- Gerhardt's Test

Blood Tests for Sugar (Glucose) Estimation

Diabetes can be accurately diagnosed by estimation of blood sugar.

The various tests, which are used, for estimating blood sugar are as follows:

Fasting Blood Sugar

After an overnight fasting of 10-14 hours, blood is taken from a vein or capillary (finger tip) and blood sugar is estimated using reagent kits by either.

- Enzyme-Linked-Immunosorbent Assay (ELISA) technique.
- Radio-Immunossay (RIA) technique.
- Dip-sticks similar to that used for urine examination.

Value of this Test

- This test alone cannot be used for diagnosing diabetes.
- In mild cases this test may be normal and diabetes may be missed.
- Reliability of this test is less because true fasting cannot be assured. People invariably make the mistake of having a cup of tea/coffee before the test.
- Normal fasting value of venous blood is 100mg% and a value more than 126mg% is mostly confirmatory of the disease.

Post-Prandial (P.P) Sugar

This test is based on the principle that after carbohydrate meal or glucose ingestion, blood sugar returns to fasting level within 2 to $2^1/_2$ hours.

The earliest evidence of carbohydrate tolerance to diabetes is a delay in the return of blood sugar values to fasting level.

This test is done 2 hours after a meal or after giving 75gm glucose powder in 300ml of water.

Value of this Test

- This is a better guide than fasting levels for diagnosing diabetes.
- Normal value is 200mg% and values above 200mg% indicates presence of diabetes.

- High values are seen in following conditions:

Prolonged inactivity, carbohydrate deprivation, excessive fat intake, liver disorder, menstrual period, advanced age and certain medicines like steroids, oral pills, sleeping pills.

- Low values are seen in following conditions:

After exertion, vomiting, and aspirin.

This test is also important for monitoring the control of diabetes.

If blood sample is taken 2 hours after a meal along with medicines for diabetes, the blood value gives an indication of control of the disease.

Random Blood Sugar

Random blood sugar estimation refers to the blood sample being taken at any particular time of the day especially when it does not correspond with a fasting or post-meal (prandial) state.

Value of this Test

This test only gives a very crude idea about the diabetes and has very little place in the diagnosis of diabetes.

It could be confirmatory only when values higher than 250mg% are found.

Glucose Tolerance Test (G.T.T)

Principle of this Test

This test is based on the principle that ingestion of glucose in a normal person leads to a rise in blood sugar level in $1/2$ to 1 hour and returns to fasting level within 2 to $2^1/2$ hours. In a diabetic the rise in blood sugar is greater, is sustained longer and there is a delay in returning to fasting levels.

Procedure

After an overnight fasting of 10-14 hours the person's blood is collected from a vein and repeated after 2 hours. In some cases the test may be prolonged to 3 to 4 hours. After taking the first sample in the fasting state, 75gm of glucose is dissolved in 300ml water and the test repeated every ½ hour for 2 hours.

This test should be done in a person on a normal diet and performing normal activities. During the test, the person must be at physical and mental rest and should not smoke. The values of this test in normal and diabetic individuals are given below.

G.T.T. Values for Normal and Diabetic Individuals

	Normal (mg%)	Borderline (mg%)	Diabetes (mg%)
Fasting	<110	110-125 (IFG)	> 126
After 2 hours	<140	140-199 (IGT)	≥ 200

NB: IFG – Impaired fasting glucose

IGT – Impaired glucose tolerance

These are intermediate stages of diabetes.

Value of this Test

- This test is a very useful one and gives almost fool proof diagnosis of diabetes.

- It is also useful in detecting borderline cases of diabetes that will eventually develop diabetes.

- It is not used these days because it is time-consuming and at times very ill, debilitated patients cannot undergo such a tedious test in a laboratory or hospital.

- Various factors affect the normal values of this test (Refer P.P. sugar).

Dextrometer/Glucometer

Certain portable devices are available which facilitate diagnosis and monitoring of diabetes in the doctor's clinic or even at home. Such devices are called as glucometer or dextrometer.

How to use Dextrometer/Glucometer

The person's blood is taken from the fingertip just one or two drops and applied to a tiny strip with a chemical coated pad at one end (Dextrostix, Hemoglukotest). This is then inserted into the dextrometer, which displays a digital reading of the blood sugar.

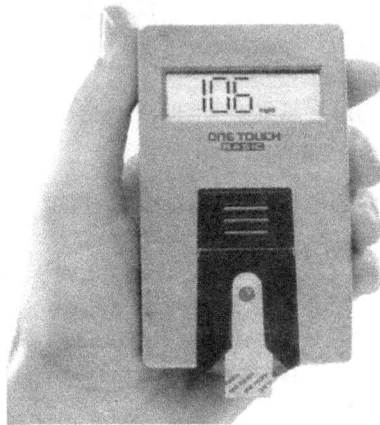

Fig. 6.1: Glucometer

Advantages and Disadvantages

This is a very reliable and a quick method of estimating blood sugar levels. This is especially useful for regular monitoring as in the case of newly diagnosed cases where dosage of medicines has to be adjusted initially. Patients with Type 1 and uncontrolled diabetes have to undergo blood tests 2-3 times a day and going to the laboratory several times a day may be difficult and time-consuming.

In cases of emergencies like low blood sugar and keto-acidosis especially and on holidays when the laboratory facilities are not available, this procedure becomes handy.

In elderly, bed-ridden patients and pregnant women who are not very mobile, the dextrometer is very useful.

Presently the dextrometer and the strips used are quite expensive, though cost may be reduced after import of various components is replaced by indigenous manufacture.

Glycosylated Haemoglobin

Haemoglobin is an iron containing substance found in our red blood cells and combines with oxygen and transports it to various body organs. Sometimes glucose gets attached to haemoglobin, the molecule being named glycosylated haemoglobin. The concentration of this glycosylated haemoglobin is a very good index of average glucose content in diabetics. It is higher in diabetic patients than normal individuals. Since each red blood cell has a life span of about 3 months, the value obtained gives an indication of blood glucose concentration of the past 3 months.

Value of this Test

- This is a very valuable test in diabetic pregnancy since it gives indication of metabolic control during pregnancy, which is important, since abnormal babies and death rate in foetuses can be minimized by proper sugar control.

- By knowing sugar control in last 3 months, modification in treatment can be done if necessary, thus long-term monitoring is possible.

- It is very useful for Insulin-dependent Diabetes where the fluctuation in blood-glucose is wide.

- Patient does not have to fast or go for test after a meal.

- It is not useful for diagnosing low-blood sugar or keto-acidosis.

- Day-to-day monitoring and treatment alteration is not possible.

- This can only by done in a good laboratory set-up.

- Unstable compound called pre-glycosylated haemoglobin can interfere with the results.

- In patients with anaemia, who have reduced haemoglobin and red blood cells, the value will be false.

- In patients with kidney com plications the values may be misleading.

Differences Between Urine and Blood Sugar Tests

Urine sugar tests	Blood sugar tests
1. Urine sugar is present only when blood sugar is more than 180 gm%.	Various values of blood sugar can be detected.
2. Useful only for diagnosing advanced diabetes.	Early and mild diabetes can even be diagnosed.
3. Other sugars (lactose, fructose etc.) may interfere and give positive sugar reactions.	Results not affected by other sugars.
4. Medicines like vitamin C, aspirin etc. may interfere with the results.	Do not interfere except when dipsticks are used.
5. In children collection of urine sample is difficult.	Collection of blood is painful but possible.
6. Emotional factors do not interfere during test.	May interfere during the test.
7. It is not an accurate method of monitoring.	It is an accurate method of monitoring diabetes control.

■ ■ ■

SELF-IMPROVEMENT/PERSONALITY DEVELOPMENT

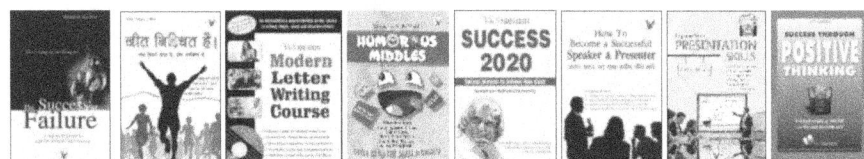

Also Available
in Hindi

Also Available
in Hindi

Also Available
in Kannada, Tamil

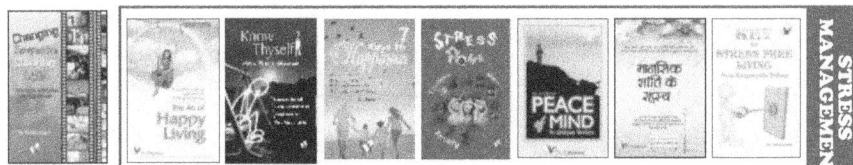

Also Available
in Kannada

Also Available
in Kannada

All books available at www.vspublishers.com